ALTERNATOR BOOKS™

INDIGENOUS ENVIRONMENTALISM

Honoring Our Relationships and Responsibilities with Nature

KATRINA M. PHILLIPS

Lerner Publications ◆ Minneapolis

To Leo and Max

Content consultant: Jill Doerfler

Lerner Publications Company
An imprint of Lerner Publishing Group, Inc.
241 First Avenue North
Minneapolis, MN 55401 USA

For reading levels and more information, look up this title at www.lernerbooks.com.

Main body text set in Aptifer Sans LT Pro Medium.
Typeface provided by Linotype AG.

Designer: Athena Currier **Photo Editor:** Nicole Berglund
Lerner team: Connie Kuhnz

Map illustration on page 20 by Laura K. Westlund

Library of Congress Cataloging-in-Publication Data

Names: Phillips, Katrina M., author.
Title: Indigenous environmentalism : honoring our relationships and responsibilities with nature / Katrina M. Phillips.
Description: Minneapolis : Lerner Publications , 2024. | Series: Native rights (Alternator Books) | Includes bibliographical references and index. | Audience: Ages 8–12 | Audience: Grades 4–6 | Summary: "From controlled burns to protesting pipelines, Indigenous peoples have always stood for their rights and the rights of nature. Discover how Native Americans are reclaiming cultural lands and taking care of them"—Provided by publisher.
Identifiers: LCCN 2023038309 (print) | LCCN 2023038310 (ebook) | ISBN 9798765625545 (library binding) | ISBN 9798765629154 (paperback) | ISBN 9798765635926 (epub)
Subjects: LCSH: Indian environmentalists—United States—Juvenile literature. | Environmental protection—United States—Citizen participation—Juvenile literature.
Classification: LCC GE197 .P526 2024 (print) | LCC GE197 (ebook) | DDC 363.7/05008997073—dc23/eng/20231011

LC record available at https://lccn.loc.gov/2023038309
LC ebook record available at https://lccn.loc.gov/2023038310

Manufactured in the United States of America
1-1010126-51888-11/7/2023

TABLE OF CONTENTS

INTRODUCTION
PROTECTING THE RIGHTS OF NATURE

On August 4, 2021, the White Earth Band of Ojibwe sued the Minnesota Department of Natural Resources (DNR). White Earth said the DNR was hurting manoomin. Manoomin is also known as wild rice. It means "good berry" in Ojibwemowin, the Ojibwe language.

Wild rice is part of the Ojibwe's creation story. Hundreds of years ago, Ojibwe people lived on the land that is now the United States' East Coast. A prophecy told them to go west until they found food growing on the water. They traveled until they reached Gichigami, also called Lake Superior. At the lake, wild rice was growing on the water. Since then Ojibwe nations have honored wild rice as a gift from the Creator and have a responsibility to take care of it.

During the 1800s, Ojibwe nations signed treaties with the US. These treaties promised that Ojibwe people would continue to hunt, fish, and gather wild rice in their homelands forever.

In 2018 White Earth passed a law to protect wild rice. Three years later, the Canadian multinational company Enbridge wanted to rebuild the Line 3 oil pipeline. Pipelines are lines of underground pipes that move gas or oil. The old Line 3 was cracking.

Enbridge wanted to pump up 5 billion gallons (19 billion L) of groundwater to build the new Line 3. The pipeline was going to be built close to where wild rice grows. White Earth said Line 3 would hurt wild rice since it needs water to grow.

They sued the DNR for the rights of wild rice. Ojibwe people, like many other Indigenous peoples, believe plants, animals, and the natural world should have the same rights people do. The White Earth lawsuit is considered the first US tribal court case that focuses on nature's rights.

Wild rice grows on Rice Lake in Minnesota.

CHAPTER 1
Looking to the Past

Historically, the land gave Indigenous peoples everything they needed. People on the Great Plains hunted for buffalo. Great Lakes people harvested manoomin and trapped beavers. People living by water fished. Others hunted for whales or seals. Some people followed the animals as they traveled. Others grew crops such as corn, beans, and squash.

Indigenous peoples made sure not to take more than they needed. If they hunted for buffalo, they tried to use every part of the buffalo. They took care of the land because the land took care of them.

A citizen of the Karuk Tribe uses a net to fish for salmon in 2014.

Caring for the Land

Sometimes taking care of the land meant changing it. Indigenous peoples have practiced cultural burning for centuries. They would set small, controlled fires to help food grow. Controlled burns also prevented bigger fires. Controlled fires helped create better habitats for animals. One of the animals this helped is a bird whose feathers were used in ceremonial clothing. So burns were ceremonially important too.

They also let fires that started on their own die out on their own. This helps the soil stay healthy. It also encourages the growth of certain plants such as milkweed or plants used for weaving baskets.

A woman from the Seminole Tribe of Florida shows children how to weave a basket.

Many Indigenous nations believe nature has its own rights. This is not something the US government recognizes. What do you believe? Why?

Land and Treaties

After the US was created, government officials wanted more Indigenous lands. They wanted lands to sell to their people so they could live there. The US believed land was something a person should own. Most Indigenous nations used the land to help the community.

The Treaty of Fort Wayne was signed in 1809. It took 2.5 million acres (1 million ha) of land from the Potawatomi, Delaware, Miami, and Eel River Nations.

The US government started making treaties with Indigenous nations in the late 1700s. Indigenous nations often sold lands to the US but kept certain rights to use the land. In many cases, the US government forced Indigenous peoples onto reservations. US officials stopped some traditional Indigenous practices such as controlled burning.

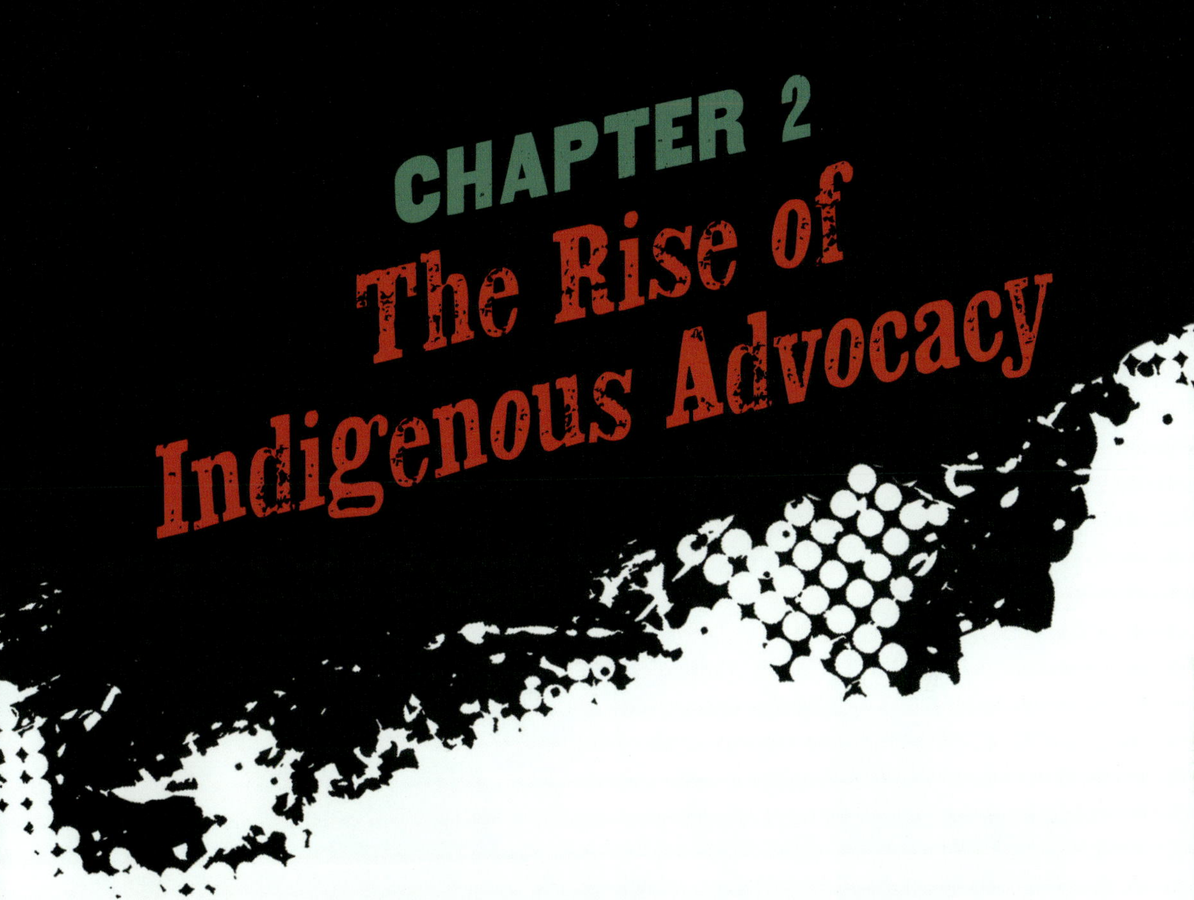

CHAPTER 2
The Rise of Indigenous Advocacy

The US government turned some Indigenous lands into national parks. The first national park, Yellowstone National Park, was created in 1872. More parks followed, such as Yosemite, Glacier, and Zion.

Taos Blue Lake

Sometimes the government took sacred Indigenous sites, such as Taos Blue Lake. Taos Blue Lake is the most sacred site for Taos Pueblo people. They see it as the source of life. It is important for their religious ceremonies and rituals. The US made Taos Blue Lake part of the Carson National Forest in New Mexico in 1906.

The Taos Pueblo spent decades fighting for the return of Taos Blue Lake. They asked Congress for a hearing. They filed

Pueblo elder Paul Bernal (*left*) and Taos elder Juan de Jesus Romero (*center*) watch as a law is signed returning Blue Lake to the Taos Pueblo peoples in 1970.

a suit with the Indian Claims Commission. They asked national organizations for support. In 1970 Congress passed a law returning Blue Lake to the Taos Pueblo.

REFLECT

US national parks were often created on lands held by Indigenous nations and overseen by the US government. How do you think this may have affected Indigenous ceremonies and cultural practices?

The Kinzua Dam was built in 1965 despite protests from the Seneca Nation of Indians.

Flooded Lands

The US government also flooded Indigenous lands. The Kinzua Dam flooded more than 15 square miles (40 sq. km) of the Allegany Territory of the Seneca Nation of Indians. The Oahe Dam flooded more than 312 square miles (809 sq. km) on the Cheyenne River Reservation and the Standing Rock Sioux Reservation. The Fort Randall Dam flooded more than 33 square miles (87 sq. km) of Indigenous lands. But Indigenous nations and peoples did not back down.

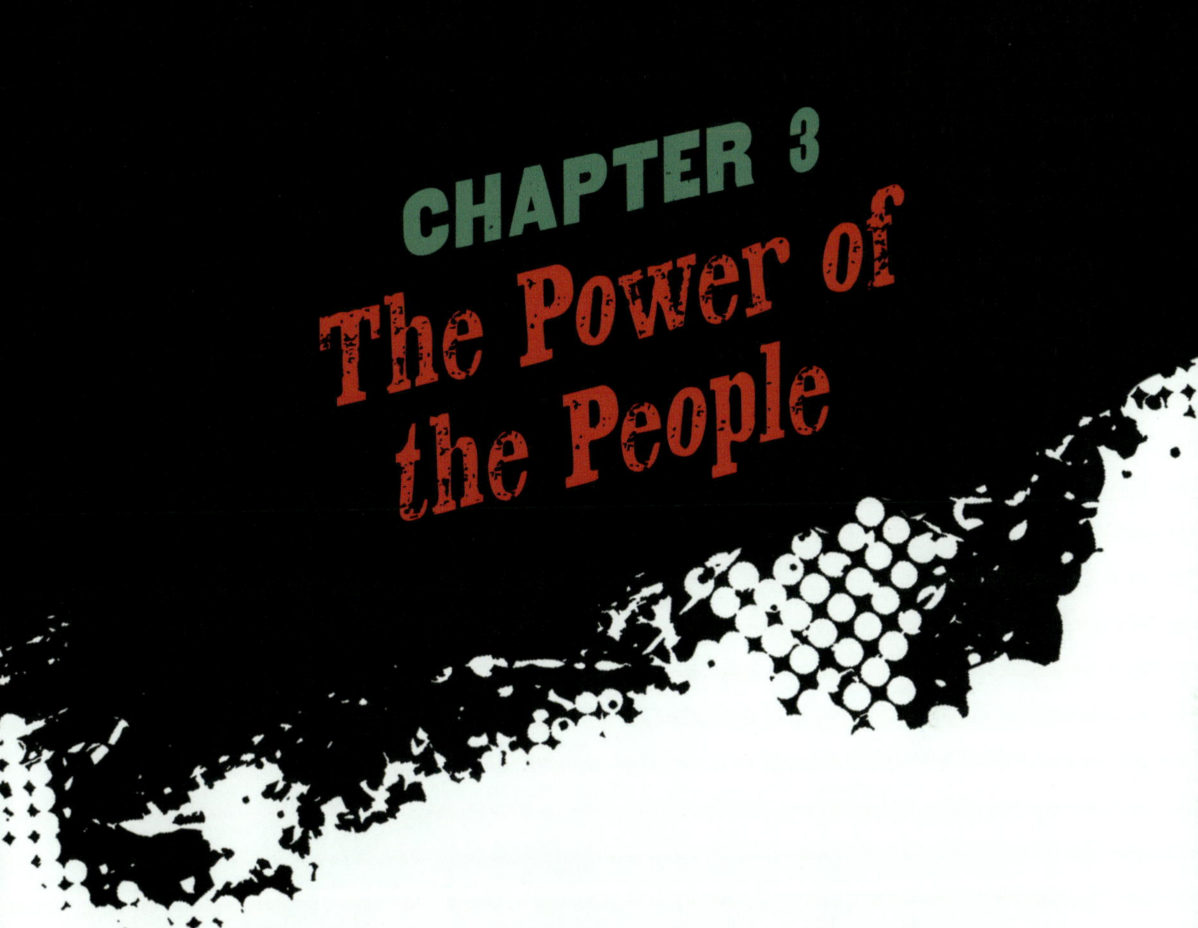

CHAPTER 3 The Power of the People

Indigenous peoples speak up for the environment and their rights to tribal sovereignty. They protest against pipelines. When pipelines leak or spill, it hurts the environment. In 1991 the Line 3 pipeline spilled 1.7 million gallons (6.4 million L) of oil in Minnesota.

#NoDAPL

The #NoDAPL protest began in 2016. Energy Transfer Partners wanted to build a pipeline. It would run from northwestern North Dakota through South Dakota and Iowa to Illinois. The project was called the Dakota Access Pipeline. It was going

Over a thousand people protest the Dakota Access Pipeline in 2016.

to run through Bismarck, North Dakota. But white residents feared their water would be harmed. So the company moved the route north of the Standing Rock Sioux Reservation. The Standing Rock Sioux Tribe stood for the land and against the pipeline. They said the pipeline threatened their water supply and cultural resources. The pipeline also violated an 1868 treaty that said Indigenous nations had a right to that land.

In April 2016, the US Army said the pipeline would not hurt historic sites. But an army archaeologist found five cultural sites that would be harmed. More than thirty other historic sites are nearby. Standing Rock sued the army in August 2016. Only a month later construction crews destroyed an area that included ancestral gravesites and prayer sites.

AUTUMN PELTIER

Autumn Peltier is an Indigenous water protector. She is from the Wiikwemkoong First Nation on Manitoulin Island in Ontario, Canada. At the age of twelve, she spoke at a 2016 meeting of the Assembly of First Nations. Her talk inspired the Niabi Odacidae fund. The fund helps protect water sources. She became chief water commissioner for the Anishinabek Nation in 2019.

In 2023 Peltier speaks about water's rights and honoring Indigenous peoples.

Bobbi Jean Three Legs (*second from left*) is a citizen of the Standing Rock Nation Sioux Tribe. She led several runs to protest the pipeline.

The US government signed treaties with Indigenous nations that promised to protect Indigenous rights. How do you think Indigenous nations and peoples exercise their treaty rights in modern times?

Indigenous and non-Indigenous peoples came from across the country to show their support. They also set up camps to stop the pipeline from being built. More than 140,000 people signed a petition to the army.

Young people from the Oceti Sakowin Youth & Allies ran a traditional relay run from the Standing Rock Reservation to Washington, DC, in September 2016. They ran 2,000 miles (3,219 km) with the petition. They started in Standing Rock Reservation and brought it to Washington, DC. Historically, Indigenous peoples used these runs to share messages across long distances.

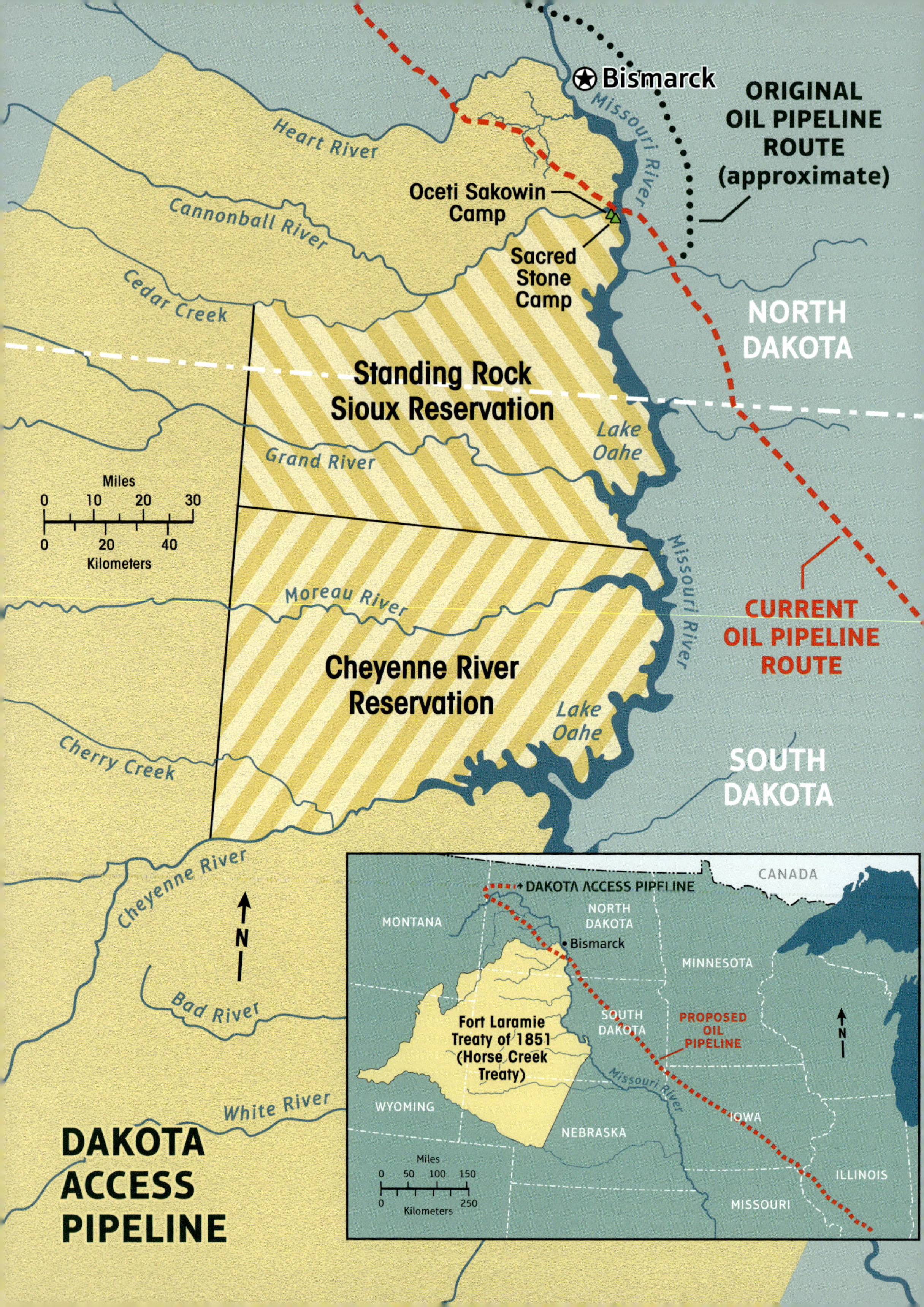

Bismarck
ORIGINAL OIL PIPELINE ROUTE (approximate)
Heart River
Missouri River
Oceti Sakowin Camp
Sacred Stone Camp
Cannonball River
Cedar Creek
NORTH DAKOTA
Standing Rock Sioux Reservation
Lake Oahe
Grand River
Miles
0 10 20 30
0 20 40
Kilometers
Missouri River
CURRENT OIL PIPELINE ROUTE
Moreau River
Cheyenne River Reservation
Lake Oahe
Cherry Creek
SOUTH DAKOTA
Cheyenne River
N
Bad River
White River
DAKOTA ACCESS PIPELINE
CANADA
DAKOTA ACCESS PIPELINE
MONTANA
NORTH DAKOTA
Bismarck
MINNESOTA
SOUTH DAKOTA
Fort Laramie Treaty of 1851 (Horse Creek Treaty)
PROPOSED OIL PIPELINE
N
Missouri River
WYOMING
NEBRASKA
IOWA
ILLINOIS
MISSOURI
Miles
0 50 100 150
0 250
Kilometers

People protest the Dakota Access Pipeline near the Standing Rock Sioux Reservation on August 12, 2016.

The pipeline company hired security guards so the construction would continue. Jack Dalrymple, then governor of North Dakota, sent the National Guard to the site. In November 2016, police officers used tear gas and water cannons to force water protectors to leave.

Standing Rock and the Cheyenne River Sioux Tribe asked the US District Court to stop the last part of the pipeline. But the court said no.

Doug Burgum, the new governor, ordered all protesters to leave by February 22, 2017. Many people left on their own. Some stayed and were arrested. Indigenous peoples and their allies were not able to stop the pipeline from being built. But they brought international attention to the unequal environmental problems that Indigenous peoples face.

NATIVE AND INDIGENOUS ADVOCACY GROUPS

Advocacy groups help protect Indigenous rights and the rights of nature. The Native American Rights Fund offers legal aid to Native nations and groups. Honor the Earth and the Indigenous Environmental Network raise awareness for Indigenous environmental justice. Indigenous Climate Action brings Indigenous peoples together around climate change.

Dallas Goldtooth leads a campaign to stop using fossil fuels as part of the Indigenous Environmental Network. In 2015 he spoke in Paris, France, about the need to stop using fossil fuels.

Nibi Walks

Many Indigenous nations use their ceremonies to advocate for change. Ojibwe grandmothers lead Nibi Walks. *Nibi* means "water" in Ojibwemowin. These walks honor all water. They also bring attention to threats water faces. People on the Nibi Walks offer songs and prayers for the water. They carry water with them until they reach the end of the route. They pour the water they carried into the lake or river at the end of the route. In August 2023, they led a Nibi Walk around Gichigami. They want to protect the lake for future generations.

Gichigami is one of the world's largest freshwater lakes.

CHAPTER 4
Looking to the Future

A fire started on Stockton Island in northern Wisconsin in 2017. The fire had been set to help the island's land and make more blueberries grow. The island's Ojibwe name is Wiisaakodewan-minis, which means "the place that has been burned." Ojibwe leaders worked hard to bring back the controlled burns after many years.

The Return of Burns

Indigenous practices such as controlled, cultural burns are part of Traditional Ecological Knowledge. Cultural burns are becoming more common across the US. In 2022 controlled

Big Cypress National Preserve and Everglades National Park after a controlled burn in 2009

burns occurred in Florida's Big Cypress National Preserve and Everglades National Park. These burns help protect endangered animals' habitats and guard against wildfires. State and federal departments worked with Native American nations for these burns. Seminole and Miccosukee peoples help care for such places as Big Cypress.

Without cultural burning, leaves and other material build up on the forest floors. Then wildfires spread more easily. These fires can destroy large trees and animals' habitats.

Helping Water Flow

Indigenous peoples are also restoring water's natural flow. In 2022 a federal agency approved their requests to remove four dams on the Klamath River. The dams were built on the Yurok,

The Iron Gate Dam is one of the dams that will be removed on the Klamath River.

An elder of the Yurok Tribe talks at a protest about removing the dams along the Klamath River in 2016.

Klamath, and Karuk lands between 1918 and 1962. The dams stopped salmon from going back to the rivers and streams where they lay their eggs. The Yurok, Hoopa Valley, Klamath, and Karuk depend on salmon, but they have not been able to fish because of the dams. The dams also slowed the river's current. The water heated up and created more algae, bacteria, and parasites. This caused more than sixty thousand salmon to die in 2002. When the dams are down, advocates

Citizens of the Standing Rock Sioux Tribe and supporters protest to protect water in 2017.

hope the river can return to its natural state and the salmon can return to their homes.

Indigenous peoples have always advocated for the environment. Their relationships with the land and the water shape cultural practices. They honor and respect the land and protect it for future generations.

REFLECT

Many reservations are at a higher risk of being affected by climate change. Why might this be? What are some of the potential consequences?

Glossary

advocate: the practice of creating awareness around an issue and campaigning for change

climate change: a change in the temperatures and usual weather in a particular place, caused by humans and the burning of fossil fuels

national park: protected land set aside by the federal government. In the United States, the National Park Service has overseen national parks since 1916.

reservation: in the US, an area of land held and governed by Native nations. There are more than three hundred reservations in the US.

Traditional Ecological Knowledge: the knowledge, beliefs, and practices of Indigenous peoples about the environment. Traditional Ecological Knowledge includes the relationships between people, plants, animals, and their environments. It is also part of conservation and natural resource management.

treaty: an official document signed between two or more sovereign nations

tribal sovereignty: the idea that Native Americans and Alaska Natives in the United States have the right to govern themselves. Their nations are recognized as governments by the US Constitution.

water protector: a person who works to defend and protect water and water systems around the world

Learn More

Doerfler, Jill, and Matthew J. Martinez. *Deb Haaland: First Native American Cabinet Secretary*. Minneapolis: Lerner Publications, 2023.

Gehl, Laura. *Climate Warriors: Fourteen Scientists and Fourteen Ways We Can Save Our Planet*. Minneapolis: Millbrook Press, 2023.

Indigenous Women's Water Sisterhood
https://sites.google.com/d.umn.edu/wfsmythe/home/indigenous-womens-water-sisterhood

Keene, Adrienne. *Notable Native People: 50 Indigenous Leaders, Dreamers, and Changemakers from Past and Present*. Emeryville, CA: Ten Speed, 2021.

Klein, Naomi. *How to Change Everything: The Young Human's Guide to Protecting the Planet and Each Other*. With Rebecca Stefoff. New York: Atheneum Books for Young Readers, 2021.

Native Knowledge 360°—"Treaties Still Matter: The Dakota Access Pipeline"
https://americanindian.si.edu/nk360/plains-treaties/dapl

Phillips, Katrina M. *Indigenous Peoples: Women Who Made a Difference*. New York: Children's Press, 2023.

Zinn Education Project—Native American Activism: 1960s to Present
https://www.zinnedproject.org/materials/native-american-activism-1960s-to-present/

Index

Photo Acknowledgments

Image credits: AP Photo/Dan Gunderson/Minnesota Public Radio, p. 5; AP Photo/Terray Sylvester/VWPics, p. 7; Jeff Greenberg/Getty Images, p. 8; AP Photo/Kevin Wolf/AP Images for National Museum of the American Indian, p. 10; HUM Images/Getty Images, p. 12; JimVallee/Getty Images, p. 14; Pacific Press/Getty Images, p. 16; Harry Murphy/Getty Images, p. 17; Rob Kim/Getty Images, p. 18; AP Photo/James MacPherson, p. 21; Kristian Buus/Alamy, p. 22; Claude LeTien/Getty Images, p. 23; Michael Patrick O'Neill/Alamy, p. 25; AP Photo/Gillian Flaccus, p. 26; AP Photo/The Oregonian, Benjamin Brink, p. 27; Anadolu Agency/Getty Images, p. 28. Design elements: Kiwihug/Unsplash; Miloje/Shutterstock; Archiwiz/Shutterstock; galacticus/Shutterstock; Forgem/Shutterstock; mikesj11/Shutterstock.